# An Analysis of
# Selected Poetry
## by
# William Butler Yeats
## between 1918 and 1928

### His secret lover,
### their illegitimate son
### and her murder

### Patricia Hughes

Published by Hues Books 2014

© Patricia Hughes

ISBN 9781909275089

# Table of Contents

# Introduction

This was the first book I wrote in 2006 about the relationship between my father's parents, both unknown to me or to him. I had been trying to find out about my grandmother, Lily O'Neill or Honor Bright, for twenty years, but everything about her was very obscure; there were no photographs, letters, or family details, no people she had known.

In January 2006 I saw a picture of William Butler Yeats and realised his resemblance to my father, and then his family's resemblance to my family, so I recommenced my search for my grandmother beginning with all my father had: two cuttings from a newspaper, police photographs of the murder victim and the bullet that killed her.

My father's birth certificate names his mother as Lizzie O'Neill and gives her address as 2 Catherine Street in Dublin, where he grew up himself. (Not the current Catherine Street; the original was pulled down in the 1940s.) It was off the Coombe, the main road in the Liberties. Number 2 was a seventeenth century mansion that had degenerated into tenements, with one family per room.

No owner is recorded by Dublin City Council, which may mean that the family that built it still owned it. A local greengrocer collected rents. My father grew up here with his foster mother and her 'family', a First World War veteran and his son. During his early years his own mother lived above; the newspaper shows that she later had a different address in the vicinity.

For the first few years I attempted to get information from the Garda Síochana headquarters in Dublin Castle, until I realised that they had very good reasons not to divulge anything about the murder of my grandmother nine decades previously. I had been using all kinds of sources such as Register offices and the International Genealogical Index, newspapers and biographies before I came to the conclusion that Yeats himself had nothing to do with the murder.

He was suddenly faced with a fait accompli by his wife George, who had requested the elimination of Lily, and by Kevin O'Higgins, the Minister of Justice. O'Higgins had carried out the interrogation and murder of Lily using Leopold Dillon, a Garda Superintendent, as assassin, and using Garda Chief Superintendent Colonel David Neligan to cover all traces of what had been done.

This accounted for several things, such as why I had been unable to find out anything about these events from Dublin Castle Garda Archives; such as why George became Yeats's persistent editor and refused all access to many of his papers; such as Neligan's cover story of Lily's invented 'streetwalking', such as why Yeats had been forced to abandon his illegitimate son and remain with George, as a publicly visible 'happy family'. It also gave yet another reason for the murder of O'Higgins by the IRA two years later.

At the time this book was written I knew nothing of these facts, so dear readers please forgive my errors.

All poems in this book are from Daniel Albright, ed.: Everyman: The Poems: W. B. Yeats, published by J. M. Dent, London

1990, reprinted 1991, updated 1994. The date given to the right of each poem is the supposed date of composition according to Daniel Albright. However George Yeats has edited dates, names and the order of the poems beyond recognition as far as possible.

Patricia Hughes

August 2015
**'William Butler Yeats and Honor Bright'**
**Series:**

**1.    W. B. Yeats and the Murder of Honor Bright**

**2.    An Analysis of Selected Poetry by William Butler Yeats between 1918 and 1928**

**3.    Who Killed Honor Bright?**
**How William Butler and George Yeats Caused the Fall of the Irish Free State**

## Michael Robartes' dancer and who she was not

Both my father and I loved poetry; we quoted it to each other all the time. He had racks of it on his bookshelves, and he delighted in showing me the beauty and honesty of the mere arrangement of words.

Later when I saw a picture of William Butler Yeats being awarded the Nobel Prize I knew I'd seen it years before, perhaps as a child. And somehow I knew some of his poetry before I read it.

The point about poetry, my father used to say, is that you can't pretend. It has to come from the heart, in the same way that a painting reflects your true colours dictated by your emotions. It talks about something rational. but has to include the warmth of your individual feelings, as well as the intensity of rhyme, word-association and metre to make it work.

I had a thin paperback of William Butler Yeats's verse, but hadn't read it much; I had no real understanding of what he was expressing. There were a few poems I knew well somehow, such as "The Lake Isle of Innisfree", "Wandering Aengus" and "Easter 1916", where his beautiful, evocative phrases had left their mark in my head, but I was never inclined to read all his works.

That changed in 2006, when I read his poetry systematically for the first time. One evening in January that year I had been leafing through 'The Guardian' when I came across a picture of William Butler Yeats receiving his Nobel Prize in 1923. I suddenly remembered my father, and began looking at his facial features, comparing them with my father's. They were exactly the same, except that Yeats has a longer nose and was taller.

The next day I went to the local library and found a book with pictures of Yeats's family. They looked very similar to mine. Inside the front cover was a picture of him as a young man that froze me to the spot; he was the very image of my father.

My father was an illegitimate child who did not know who his father was – although in retrospect in my opinion he did have an inkling. He had been brought up in Dublin by a foster mother, and had not discovered his real mother until required to produce a birth certificate on joining the British Army in 1942.

His real mother had been murdered when he was four years old, and maligned as a prostitute, a streetwalker; her 'reputation' had spread like fire throughout Dublin and she was still talked about. But no details were ever attached to the story, and I had found it impossible to find out about her because every attempt led to a dead end.

Now, surprisingly, I had realised that Yeats was my father's father, so my father's mother, Lily O'Neill (known by Dubliners as 'Honor Bright') must have had a love affair with him. But Yeats didn't seem the kind of man to use streetwalkers; it was very puzzling. I decided to take a good look at his poetry.

I was looking for references to his relationship with a young woman, leading to the birth of their son, brought up by another woman as her own child. I couldn't afford the 'Variorum' edition but I bought one that showed the dates when they were written.

Then I set about finding out what they could tell me about the man.

Before reading his poems I noted two pieces of information from the biographies: first, he made constant revisions to his poems even after publication, so the date of authorship is not usually as shown. Second, he was adept at manipulating words, as befits a playwright, poet and mage, so details of his private life are often deliberately made obscure. Therefore when he refers to events in his poetry he or his wife George, who acted as his editor, have often deliberately changed details.

Excerpt from "The Double Vision of Michael Robartes"

II
On the grey rock of Cashel I suddenly saw
A Sphinx with woman breast and lion paw,
A Buddha, hand at rest,
Hand lifted up that blest;

And right between these two a girl at play
That, it may be, had danced her life away,
For now being dead it seemed
That she of dancing dreamed.

Although I saw it all in the mind's eye

There can be nothing solider till I die;
I saw by the moon's light
Now at its fifteenth night.

One lashed her tail; her eyes lit by the moon
Gazed upon all things known, all things
unknown,
In triumph of intellect
With motionless head erect.

That other's moonlit eyeballs never moved,
Being fixed on all things loved, all things
unloved,
Yet little peace he had,
For those that love are sad.

O little did they care who danced between,
And little did she by whom her dance was
seen
So she had outdanced thought.
Bodily perfection brought,

For what but eye and ear silence the mind
With the minute particulars of mankind?
Mind moved yet seemed to stop
As 'twere a spinning-top.

In contemplation had those three so wrought
Upon a moment, and so stretched it out
That they, time overthrown,
Were dead yet flesh and bone.

III
I knew that I had seen, had seen at last
That girl my unremembering nights hold fast
Or else my dreams that fly
If I should rub an eye,

And yet in flying fling into my meat
A crazy juice that makes the pulses beat
As though I had been undone
By Homer's Paragon

Who never gave the burning town a thought;
To such a pitch of folly I am brought,
Being caught between the pull
Of the dark moon and the full,

The commonness of thought and images
That have the frenzy of our western seas.
Thereon I made my moan
And after kissed a stone,

And after that arranged it in a song
Seeing that I, ignorant for so long,
Had been rewarded thus
In Cormac's ruined house.

A mystery girl appears all at once in this poem in "The Wild Swans at Coole". It is dated somewhere between March - April 1918 and 1919, and talks about a real girl he has fallen in love with. Michael Robartes is an alter ego for Yeats, which he invented to make himself younger sexier and working class. The girl in the poem is a dancer, and he sees her between two people, "A Sphinx with woman breast and lion paw", and "a Buddha, hand at rest, Hand lifted up that blest;/ And right between these two a girl at play" who was completely absorbed by her dance to the point of having "outdanced thought". He cannot forget "That girl my unremembering nights hold fast", and he is affected by "A crazy juice that makes the pulses beat" that brings him to "the point of folly".

Yeats spent a year living in Stone Cottage with Ezra Pound in 1913 and they both learnt a great deal from each other; Pound learnt about rhyme and metre, while Yeats learnt to write about real life rather than fairy stories. In the last poem Yeats's wife George is the sphinx and Yeats is the Buddha. The girl between them is young: a child who plays, a dancer. He compares her to the new moon in the first stanza, and later to the "dark moon", the one that is not seen. By contrast his wife is "the old moon", "the Sphinx" who "lashed her tail; her eyes lit by the moon... In triumph of intellect." The dancer's "moonlit eyeballs never moved, being fixed on all things loved, all things unloved…" His wife is rational and the dancer is emotional, so he is drawn closer to the dancer.

"Michael Robartes and the Dancer"

He.    Opinion is not worth a rush;
In this altar-piece the knight,
Who grips his long spear so to push
That dragon through the fading light,
Loved the lady; and it's plain
The half-dead dragon was her thought,
That every morning rose again
And dug its claws and shrieked and fought.
Could the impossible come to pass
She would have time to turn her eyes,
Her lover thought, upon the glass
And on the instant would grow wise.

She.   You mean they argued.

He.                          Put it so;
But bear in mind your lover's wage
Is what your looking-glass can show,
And that he will turn green with rage
At all that is not pictured there.

She.   May I not put myself to college?

He.   Go pluck Athena by the hair;

For what mere book can grant a knowledge
With an impassioned gravity
Appropriate to that beating breast,
That vigorous thigh, that dreaming eye?
And may the devil take the rest.

She.   And must no beautiful woman be
Learned like a man?

He.                Paul Veronese
And all his sacred company
Imagined bodies all their days
By the lagoon you love so much,
For proud, soft, ceremonious proof
That all must come to sight and touch;
While Michael Angelo's Sistine roof,
His 'morning' and his 'night' disclose
How sinew that has been pulled tight,
Or it may be loosened in repose,
Can rule by supernatural right
Yet be but sinew.

She.          I have heard said
There is great danger in the body.

He.    Did God in portioning wine and bread
Give man his thought or his mere body?

She.   My wretched dragon is perplexed.

He.    I have principles to prove me right.

16

It follows from this Latin text
That blessed souls are not composite,
And that all beautiful women may
Live in uncomposite blessedness,
And lead us to the like – if they
Will banish every thought, unless
The lineaments that please their view
When the long looking-glass is full,
Even from the foot-sole think it too.

She. They say such different things at
school.

The above poem, also written in 1918, is an
intimate conversation between him and the
dancer. She has great sympathy for the
dragon, a personification of Yeats. He tells
her to look in the mirror to see her own
beauty clearly. She is dismissive and says
that she wants to go to college, but he says
her beauty is more important than books. He
is saying he loves her as she stands in front
of the mirror, and they are speaking
imtimately and intensely, alone together as
if they have just made love.

This poem is thought to be a conversation
between Yeats and Iseult Gonne, the
daughter of Maud, but it has a sexual
undercurrent. Yeats and Iseult never slept
together and were never physically in love

(although he had fantasised about her from a distance), so she was never intimate with him; he was like a father to her. Furthermore the date of the poem is inappropriate for Iseult; one year after Yeats had married George; one and a half years since Iseult had turned down his marriage proposal, and one year before she married Francis Stuart, nine years younger than herself. During 1918 Yeats and his wife were living in Dublin, while Iseult, very uninclined to study, was having an affair with Ezra Pound in London. So Yeats was not physically involved with Iseult at the time, or thinking she wanted to go to college.

The girl in the poem was young, hence the reference to her future at college. It might have been his young wife George, except that he writes in a completely different style about her, He has far less sexual drive towards her; in his poetry they are friends and partners. In his poem "Solomon and the Witch" he says

"Maybe the bride-bed brings despair
For each an imagined image brings
And finds a real image there."

Who might his imagined image have been?

Solomon and the Witch

And thus declared that Arab lady:
'Last night, where under the wild moon
On grassy mattress I had laid me,
Within my arms great Solomon,
I suddenly cried out in a strange tongue
Not his, not mine.'
                        Who understood
Whatever has been said, sighed, sung,
Howled, miau-d, barked, brayed, belled,
yelled, cried, crowed,
Thereon replied: 'A cockerel
Crew from a blossoming apple bough
Three hundred years before the Fall,
And never crew again till now,
And would not now but that he thought,
Chance being at one with Choice at last,
All that the brigand apple brought
And this foul world were dead at last.
He that crowed out eternity
Though to have crowed it in again.
For though love has a spider's eye
To find out some appropriate pain –
Aye, though all passion's in the glance –
For every nerve, and tests a lover
With cruelties of Choice and Chance;
And when at last that murder's over
Maybe the bride-bed brings despair,
For each an imagined image brings
And finds a real image there;

Yet the world ends when these two things,
Thought several, are a single light,
When oil and wick are burned in one;
Therefore a blessed moon last night
Gave Sheba to her Solomon.'
'Yet the world stays.'
                              'If that be so,
Your cockerel found us in the wrong
Although he thought it worth a crow.
Maybe an image is too strong
Or maybe is not strong enough.'

'The night has fallen; not a sound
in the forbidden sacred grove
unless a petal hit the ground,
nor any human sight within it
but the crushed grass where we have lain;
and the moon is wilder every minute.
O! Solomon! Let us try again.'


In contrast "Under Saturn", written in
November 1919, shows him very loyal to
George:

Under Saturn

Do not because this day I have grown
saturnine
Imagine that lost love, inseparable from my
thought

Because I have no other youth, can make me pine;
For how should I forget the wisdom that you brought,
The comfort that you made? Although my wits have gone
On a fantastic ride, my horse's flanks are spurred
By childish memories of an old cross Pollexfen,
And of a Middleton, whose name you never heard,
And of a red-haired Yeats whose looks, although he died
Before my time, seem like a vivid memory.
You heard that labouring man who had served my people. He said
Upon the open road, near to the Sligo quay –
No, no, not said, but cried it out – 'You have come again,
And surely after twenty years it was time to come.'
I am thinking of a child's vow sworn in vain
Never to leave that valley his fathers called their home.

This was written just after Yeats had moved to Oxford with George, so the dancer in Dublin was his 'lost love'.

Yeats's young lover could not have been Maud Gonne. His contemporary relationship with her, as revealed in "On a Political Prisoner" written 10-29 January 1919, was far from amorous.

On a Political Prisoner

She that but little patience knew,
From childhood on, had now so much
A grey gull lost its fear and flew
Down to her cell and there alit,
And there endured her fingers' touch
And from her fingers ate its bit.

Did she in touching that lone wing
Recall the years before her mind
Became a bitter, an abstract thing,
Her thought some popular enmity:
Blind and leader of the blind
Drinking the foul ditch where they lie?

When long ago I saw her ride
Under Ben Bulben to the meet,
The beauty of her country-side
With all youth's lonely wildness stirred,
She seemed to have grown clean and sweet
Like any rock-bred, sea-borne bird:

Sea-borne, or balanced on the air
When frst it sprang out of its nest

Upon some lofty rock to stare
Upon the cloudy canopy,
While under its storm-beaten breast
Cried out the hollows of the sea.

After the death of her husband John MacBride, Maud had tried to return from their residence in France to Dublin, despite being banned from Ireland by British authorities for her support of the Republican movement. So while passing through England she had been detained and imprisoned in London. Yeats, who disapproved of her political activities, wrote that she had been lovely once but now she was a different person. Her mind was "a bitter, an abstract thing", she was full of "enmity", "drinking the foul ditch"; she was "blind" and "a leader of the blind." He repeats this disapproval in "The Leaders of the Crowd" and it is also apparent in "A Prayer for My Daughter" written between 29th February and June, 1919, in that he wishes for his daughter the opposite of the life that Maud leads. At this time Gonne was 54 years old (roughly his own age) and had a grown-up daughter, Iseult. She was therefore hardly the young dancer wanting to go to college of the Michael Robartes series.

The Leaders of the Crowd

They must to keep their certainty accuse
All that are different of a base intent;
Pull down established honour; hawk for
news
Whatever their loose phantasy invent
And murmur it with bated breath, as though
The abounding gutter had been Helicon
Or calumny a song. How can they know
Truth flourishes where the student's lamp
has shone,
And there alone, that have no solitude?
So the crowd come they dare not what may
come.
They have loud music, hope every day
renewed
And heartier loves; that lamp is from the
tomb.


A Prayer For My Daughter

Once more the storm is howling, and half
hid
Under this cradle-hood and coverlid
My child sleeps on. There is no obstacle
But Gregory's wood and one bare hill
Whereby the haystack- and roof-levelling
wind,
Bred on the Atlantic, can be stayed;

And for an hour I have walked and prayed
Because of the great gloom that is in my
mind.

I have walked and prayed for this young
child an hour
And heard the sea-wind scream upon the
tower,
And under the arches of the bridge, and
scream
In the elms above the flooded stream;
Imagining in excited reverie
That the future years had come,
Dancing to a frenzied drum,
Out of the murderous innocence of the sea.

May she be granted beauty and yet not
Beauty to make a stranger's eye distraught,
Or hers before a looking-glass, for such
Being made beautiful overmuch,
Consider beauty a sufficient end,
Lose natural kindness and maybe
The heart-revealing intimacy
That chooses right, and never find a friend.

Helen being chosen found life flat and dull
And later had much trouble from a fool,
While that great Queen, that rose out of the
spray,
Being fatherless could have her way
Yet chose a bandy-leggèd smith for man.

It's certain that fine women eat
A crazy salad with their meat
Whereby the Horn of Plenty is undone.

In courtesy I'd have her chiefly learned;
Hearts are not had as a gift but hearts are
earned
By those that are not entirely beautiful;
Yet many, that have played the fool
For beauty's very self, has charm made
wise,
And many a poor man that has roved,
Loved and thought himself beloved,
From a glad kindness cannot take his eyes.

May she become a flourishing hidden tree
That all her thoughts may like the linnet be,
And have no business but dispensing round
Their magnanimities of sound,
Nor but in merriment begin a chase,
Nor but in merriment a quarrel.
O may she live like some green laurel
Rooted in one dear perpetual place.

My mind, because the minds that I have
loved,
The sort of beauty that I have approved,
Prosper but little, has dried up of late,
Yet knows that to be choked with hate
May well be of all evil chances chief.
If there's no hatred in a mind

Assault and battery of the wind
Can never tear the linnet from the leaf.

An intellectual hatred is the worst,
So let her think opinions are accursed.
Have I not seen the loveliest woman born
Out of the moth of plenty's horn,
Because of her opinionated mind
Barter that horn and every good
By quiet natures understood
For an old bellows full of angry wind?

Considering that, all hatred driven hence,
The soul recovers radical innocence
Self-appeasing, self-affrighting,
And that its own sweet will is Heaven's will.
She can, though every face should scowl
And every windy quarter howl
Or every bellows burst, be happy still.

And may her bridegroom bring her to a
house
Where all's accustomed, ceremonious;
For arrogance and hatred are the wares
Peddled in the thoroughfares.
How but in custom and in ceremony
Are innocence and beauty born?
Ceremony's a name for the rich horn,
And custom for the spreading laurel tree.

                    26 February – June 1919

So I had established that Yeats did have a young lover, who was not his wife or Maud or Iseult Gonne. The intimate relationship started in March – April 1918, six months after his marriage, coincided with his invention of Michael Robartes, and his lover was a dancer who wanted to go to college.

# An affair and the birth of a son

Nineteen Hundred and Nineteen

I
Many ingenious lovely things are gone
That seemed sheer miracle to the mutitude,
Protected from the circle of the moon
That pitches common things about. There
stood
Amid the ornamental bronze and stone
An ancient image made of olive wood –
And gone are Phidias' famous ivories
And all the golden grasshoppers and bees.

We too had many pretty toys when young;
A law indifferent to blame or praise,
To bribe or threat; habits that made old
wrong
Melt down, as it were wax in the sun's rays;
Public opinion ripening for so long
We thought it would outlive all future days.
O what fine thought we had because we
thought
That the worst rogues and rascals had died
out.

All teeth were drawn, all ancient tricks
unlearned,

And a great army but a showy thing;
What matter that no cannon has been
Turned into a ploughshare? Parliament and king
Thought that unless a little powder burned
The trumpeters might burst with trumpeting
And yet it lack all glory; and perchance
The guardsmen's drowsy chargers would not prance.

Now days are dragon-ridden, the nightmare
Rides upon sleep: a drunken soldiery
Can leave the mother, murdered at ther door,
To crawl in her own blood, and go scot-free;
The night can sweat with terror as before
We pierced our thoughts into philosophy,
And planned to bring the world under a rule,
Who are but weasels fighting in a hole.

He who can read the signs nor sink unmanned
Into the half-deceit of some intoxicant
From shallow wits; who knows no work can stand,
Whether health, wealth or peace of mind were spent
On master-work of intellect or hand,
No honour leave its mighty monument,
Has but one comfort left: all triumph would
But break upon his ghostly solitude.

But is there any comfort to be found?
Man is in love and loves what vanishes,
What more is there to say? That country
round
None dares admit, if such a thought were
his,
Incendiary or bigot could be found
To burn that stump on the Acropolis,
Or break in bits the famous ivories
Or traffic in the grasshoppers or bees.

II

When Loie Fuller's Chinese dancers
enwound
A shining web, a floating ribbon of cloth,
It seemed that a dragon of air
Had fallen among dancers, had whirled them
round
Or hurried them off on its own furious path;
So the Platonic Year
Whirls out new right and wrong,
Whirls in the old instead;
All men are dancers and their tread
Goes to the barbarous clangour of a gong.

III

Some moralist or mythological poet
Compares the solitary soul to a swan;
I am satisfied with that,

Satisfied if a troubled mirror show it,
Before that brief gleam of its life be gone,
An image of its state;
The wings half spread for flight,
The breast thrust out in pride
Whether to play, or to ride
Those winds that clamour of approaching
night.

A man in his own secret meditation
Is lost amid the labyrinth that he has made
In art or politics;
Some Platonist affirms that in the station
Where we should cast off body and trade
The ancient habit sticks,
And that if our works could
But vanish with our breath
That were a lucky death,
For triumph can but mar our solitude.

The swan has leaped into the desolate
heaven:
That image can bring wildness, bring a rage
To end all things, to end
What my laborious life imagined, even
The half-imagined, the half-written page;
O but we dreamed to mend
Whatever mischief seemed
To afflict mankind, but now
That winds of winter blow

Learn that we were crack-pated when we
dreamed.

IV

We, who seven years ago
Talked of honour and of truth,
Shriek with pleasure if we show
The weasel's twist, the weasel's tooth.

V

Come let us mock at the great
That had such burdens on the mind
And toiled so hard and late
To leave some monument behind,
Nor thought of the levelling wind.

Come let us mock at the wise;
With all those calendars whereon
They fixed old aching eyes,
They never saw how seasons run,
And now but gape at the sun.

Come let us mock at the good
That fancied goodness might be gay,
And sick of solitude
Might proclaim a holiday:
Wind shrieked – and where are they?

Mock mockers after that

That would not lift a hand maybe
To help good, wise or great
To bar that foul storm out, for we
Traffic in mockery.

VI

Violence upon the roads: violence of horses;
Some few have handsome riders, are garlanded
On delicate sensitive ear or tossing mane,
But wearied running round and round in their courses
All break and vanish, and evil gathers head:
Herodias' daughters have returned again,
A sudden blast of dusty wind and after
Thunder of feet, tumult of images,
Their purpose in the labyrinth of the wind;
And should some crazy hand dare touch a daughter
All turn with amorous cries, or angry cries,
According to the wind, for all are blind.
But now wind drops, dust settles; thereupon
There lurches past, his great eyes without thought
Under the shadow of straw-pale locks,
That insolent fiend Robert Artisson
To whom the love-lorn Lady Kyteler brought
Bronzed peacock feathers, red combs of her cocks.                    1920-21

34

Yeats wrote in "Nineteen Hundred and Nineteen" about "Some moralist or mythological poet..." who compared "... the solitary soul to a swan." Taking the swan as a description of himself, he declared "... I am satisfied with that..."

Leda and the Swan

A sudden blow: the great wings beating still
Above the staggering girl, her thighs caressed
By the dark webs, her nape caught in his bill,
He holds her helpless breast upon his breast.

How can those terrified vague fingers push
The feathered glory from her loosening thighs,
And how can body, laid in that white rush,
But feel the strange heart beating where it lies?

A shudder in the loins engenders there
The broken wall, the burning roof and tower
And Agamemnon dead.
                                        Being so caught up,
So mastered by the brute blood of the air,

Did she put on his knowledge with his power
Before the indifferent beak coud let her drop?

This poem portrays a sexual encounter between an older, more powerful, experienced man and a young virgin, in which he feels as if he is raping her (whether or not it actually happened). Taking into account the intensity of emotion and the physical detail in the text, and that Yeats only writes about actual events and emotions in his life, it is reality not myth.

It is very sexual, so not about his wife, to whom he was loyal but had no deep physical feelings, despite their children. In 1919 his poetry was overtly physical and very amorous, but not affectionate except when it concerns George. Of course Yeats did not say publicly that he had a lover because he was married. Similarly when George later had an affair with Lennox Robinson it was not made public.

"On a Picture of a Black Centaur by Edmund Dulac"

Your hooves have stamped at the black margins of the wood,

Even where horrible green parrots call and swing.
My works are all stamped down in the sultry mud.
I knew that horse-play, knew it for a murderous thing.
What wholesome sun has ripened is wholesome food to eat,
And that alone; yet I, being driven half insane
Because of some green wing, gathered old mummy wheat
In the mad, abstract dark and ground it grain by grain
And after baked it slowly in an oven; but now
I bring full-flavoured wine out of a barrel found
Where seven Ephesian topers slept and never knew
When Alexander's empire passed, they slept so sound.
Stretch out your limbs and sleep a long Saturnian sleep;
I have loved you better than my soul for all my words,
And there is none so fit to keep a watch and keep
Unwearied eyes upon those horrible green birds.

A centaur is a symbol of wanton male sexuality. Its blackness denotes covert or immoral events such as adultery, outside the light. Indeed Yeats says in the poem "Your hooves have stamped at the black margins of the wood" which means the centaur has been active outside his area, in other words adultery.

The "horrible green parrots" refer to Republicans whose colour is green and who were then parroting political demands. Thus when he says he is "…being driven half insane / Because of some green wing…" he is referring to a lover from that section of society. He admits "I knew that horse-play…" meaning sex outside marriage although he knows he "ought to have stayed with "…what wholesome sun has ripened…" in other words his wife.

Nevertheless he has "gathered old mummy wheat in the mad abstract dark". Wheat from the tombs of Egyptian mummies was said to begin to sprout centuries after, when removed from the dark and brought into the light. Yeats is talking about his potency; his seeds have sprung to life after having been dead for an age. "…In the mad, abstract dark… " refers to night, when sex happens, but also to the illicit nature of it. His use of the word "mummy" is about the pregnancies of his lover and George, which occurred 1919, 1920 and 1921. This mummy wheat has been exposed to the sun that has "...baked it..." and turned it into the "...full-flavoured wine..." of new life.

He finishes with "I have loved you better than my soul for all my words..." implying that this love has been detrimental to his soul, or morality and conscience. For this reason and because of its intensity it is not written for George. The given date of the poem, September 1920, was just before the birth of Kevin Barry O'Neill, his illegitimate son by Lily, on 9th November 1920.

"A Prayer for My Son" was said to be written in December 1921.

Bid a strong ghost stand at the head
That my Michael may sleep sound,
Nor cry, nor turn in the bed
Till his morning meal come round;
And may departing twilight keep
All dread afar till morning's back,
That his mother may not lack
Her fill of sleep.

Bid the ghost have sword in fist:
Some there are, for I avow

Such devilish things exist,
Who have planned his murder, for they
know
Of some most haughty deed or thought
That waits upon his future days,
And would through hatred of the bays
Bring that to nought.

Though You can fashion everything
From nothing every day, and teach
The morning stars to sing,
You have lacked articulate speech
To tell your simplest want, and known,
Wailing upon a woman's knee,
All of that worst ignominy
Of flesh and bone;

And when through all the town there ran
The servants of your enemy,
A woman and a man,
Unless the Holy Writings lie,
Hurried through the smooth and rough
And through the fertile and waste,
Protecting, till the danger past,
With human love.

In strong contrast to his usual analytic
demeanour this poem talks of Yeats's strong
fear that his son will be murdered. In the
second line he names his son as Michael, the
son of his marriage born on 22nd August

1921. Yeats talks in the second verse of knowing some people who want to murder him because of something he will do in the future to bring him fame or riches. "The bays" are ceremonial Roman or Greek head-wreaths of bay leaves worn by celebrated people.

However the poem does not appear to be focussed on this particular son, for in 1921 when the civil war in Ireland was in full flow, the Yeats family was living in peace in Oxford, England. In the last verse he compares the civil war in Dublin and the birth of his son to the Biblical story of Mary and Joseph journeying to Nazareth: "... when through all the town there ran / The servants of Your enemy..." or soldiers. Had he and George actually been in Dublin, and had they felt personally threatened by the violence and disorder of that place and time, this poem might have referred to the infant Michael. But though Yeats no doubt followed news of events in Ireland's capital very closely, he and his family were not involved in the war at all. Avoidance of the unrest of the Irish civil war was the reason they lived in England at that time. On the other hand infant Kevin, one year older than Michael, was in Dublin during the Civil War and was threatened by random acts of violence because he lived so near to the city centre.

The names Kevin and Michael both have two syllables with stress on the first, so one name was substituted for another in the poem. There is no evidence about when this happened or who did it, but George did most of the revisions to Yeats' poems after he married her. The woman and the man in the poem could have been Yeats and his wife mingling with the aristocracy and academics in Oxfordshire. However they were much more likely to be Margaret Magill and James White who were raising Kevin as their foster-child alongside White's own son. Yeats was indisputably terrified about danger to one of his male offspring. This poem could have been written in December 1920 because that was one month after baby Kevin was born in Dublin. George Yeats who later 'edited' Yeats' works may have changed the dates. In adult life Michael said that he was intensely embarrassed by this poem, which he did not understand at all.

The "most haughty deed or thought" was prior birth, since Kevin was born ten months before Michael. Yeats' anxiety about what will happen to his property is also present in

"Meditations in Time of Civil War", written 1921. Here is an excerpt:

".... Out of life's own self-delight had sprung
the abounding glittering jet; though now it seems
As if some marvellous empty sea-shell flung
Out of the obscure dark of the rich streams,
And not a fountain, were the symbol which
Shadows the inherited glory of the rich. ..."

The title of the poem sets it "... in time of Civil War"; but it talks of his anxiety about legal claims of inheritance to his property rather than violence by marauders. The two parts of it are "Ancestral Houses" and "My House". The "fountain" is legitimate offspring, while the "empty sea-shell flung out of the obscure dark of the rich streams" is an accidental product, an illegitimate child. Yeats is describing the abject contrast between his gracious life and that of Lily and his illegitimate son, and feeling 'bitterness'. The involvement of the poem with Civil War is restricted to the time in which he wrote it. In fact he writes one stanza about a volunteer (republican) and an affable irregular (unionist) and treats them completely alike without taking sides. His erstwhile political slogan of 'Unity of

Being' encompasses all political, religious and social divides within Ireland.

Meditation in Time of Civil War

I    Ancestral Houses

Surely among a rich man's flowering lawns,
Amid the rustle of his planted hills,
Life overflows without ambitious pains;
And rains down life until the basket spills,
And mounts more dizzy high the more it rains
As though to choose whatever shape it wills
And never stoop to a mechanical
Or servile shape, at other's beck and call.

Mere dreams, mere dreams! Yet Homer had not sung
Had he not found it certain beyond dreams
That out of life's own self-delight had sprung
The abounding, glittering jet; though now it seems
As if some marvellous empty sea-shell flung
Out of the obscure dark of the rich streams,
And not a fountain, were the symbol which
Shadows the inherited glory of the rich.

Some violent bitter man, some powerful man

Called architect and artist in, that they,
Bitter and violent men, might rear in stone
The sweetness that all longed for night and
day,
The gentleness none there had ever known;
But when the master's buried mice can play,
And maybe the great-grandson of that
house,
For all its bronze and marble, 's but a
mouse.

O what if gardens where the peacock strays
With delicate feet upon old terraces,
Or else all Juno from an urn displays
Before the indifferent garden deities;
O what if levelled lawns and gravelled ways
Where slippered Contemplation finds his
ease
And Childhood a delight for every sense,
But take our greatness with our violence?

What if the glory of escutcheoned doors,
And buildings that a haughtier age designed,
The pacing to and fro on polished floors
Amid great chambers and long galleries,
lined
With famous portraits of our ancestors;
What if those things the greatest of mankind
Consider most to magnify, or to bless,
But take our greatness with our bitterness?

# Sudden death

In "Two Songs from a Play", the first song was supposedly written in May 1925; on June 9th Lily was murdered. He speaks of his immense grief at her death, and portrays Lily as Helen of Troy because she has unwittingly provoked evil. Yeats sees "...a staring virgin stand" ... "And tear the heart out of his side / And lay the heart upon her hand / and bear that beating heart away." He has lost his heart to this "fierce virgin", and the "Odour of blood" has destroyed all his work by making "... all Platonic tolerance vain / And vain all Doric discipline." He blames himself for this tragedy: "Whatever flames upon the night / Man's own resinous heart has fed."

Two Songs from a Play
I
I saw a staring virgin stand
Where holy Dionysus died,
And tear the heart out of his side,
And lay the heart upon her hand
And bear that beating heart away;
And then did all the Muses sing
Of Magnus Annus at the spring,

As though God's death were but a play.

Another Troy must rise and set,
Another lineage feed the crow,
Another Argo's painted prow
Drive to a flashier bauble yet.
The Roman Empire stood appalled:
It dropped the reins of peace and war
When that fierce virgin and her star
Out of the fabulous darkness called.

II
In pity for man's darkening thought
He walked that room and issued thence
In Galilean turbulence;
The Babylonian starlight brought
A fabulous, formless darkness in;
Odour of blood when Christ was slain
Made all Platonic tolerance vain
And vain all Doric discipline.
                    May 1925

Everything that man esteems
Endures a moment or a day.
Love's pleasure drives his love away,
The painter's brush consumes his dreams;
The herald's cry, the soldier's tread
Exhaust his fury and his might:
Whatever flames upon the night
Man's own resinous heart has fed.
                    1930-31

"The Tower" was written on 7th October 1925, four months after the murder of Lily when his illegitimate son was four years old. His romantic but seasonally uninhabitable house was called Thoor Ballylee (Ballylee Tower), but the Tower is also a Tarot card that predicts collapse, disaster and ruin. Yeats, master of the occult, was aware of both connotations and Yeats the poet used both meanings.

The Tower
I
What shall I do with this absurdity –
O heart, O troubled heart – this caricature,
Decrepit age that has been tied to me
As to a dog's tail?
                    Never had I more
Excited, passionate, fantastical
Imagination, nor an ear and eye
That more expected the impossible –
No, not in boyhood when with rod and fly,
Or the humbler worm, I climbed Ben Bulben's back
And had the livelong summer day to spend.
It seems that I must bid the Muse go pack,
Choose Plato and Plotinus for a friend
Until imagination, ear and eye,
Can be content with argument and deal

In abstract things; or be derided by
A sort of battered kettle at the heel.

II
I pace upon the battlements and stare
On the foundations of a house, or where
Tree, like a sooty finger, starts from the
earth;
And send imagination forth
Under the day's declining beam, and call
Images and memories
From ruin or from ancient trees,
For I would ask a question of them all.

Beyond that ridge lived Mrs French, and
once
When every silver candlestick or sconce
Lit up the dark mahogany and the wine,
A serving-man, that could divine
That most respected lady's every wish,
Ran and with the garden shears
Clipped an insolent farmer's ears
And brought them in a little covered dish.

Some few remembered still when I was
young
A peasant girl commended by a song,
Who'd lived somewhere upon that rocky
place,
And praised the colour of her face,
And had the greater joy in praising her,

Remembering that, if walked she there,
Farmers jostled at the fair
So great a glory did the song confer.

And certain men, being maddened by those
rhymes,
Or else by toasting her a score of times,
Rose from the table and declared it right
To test their fancy by their sight;
But they mistook the brightness of the moon
For the prosaic light of day –
Music had driven their wits astray –
And one was drowned in the great bog of
Cloone.

Strange, but the man who made the song
was blind;
Yet, now I have considered it, I find
That nothing strange; the tragedy began
With Homer that was a blind man,
And Helen has all living hearts betrayed.
O may the moon and sunlight seem
One inextricable beam,
For if I triumph I must make men mad.

And I myself created Hanrahan
And drove him drunk or sober through the
dawn
From somewhere in the neighbouring
cottages;
Caught by an old man's juggleries

He stumbled, tumbled, fumbled to and fro
And had but broken knees for hire
And horrible splendour of desire;
I thought it all out twenty years ago:

Good fellows shuffled cards in an old bawn;
And when that ancient ruffian's turn was on
He so bewitched the cards under his thumb
That all but the one card became
A pack of hounds and not a pack of cards,
And that he changed into a hare.
Hanrahan rose in frenzy there
And followed up those baying creatures
towards –

O towards I have forgotten what – enough!
I must recall a man that neither love
Nor music nor an enemy's clipped ear
Could, he was so harried, cheer;
A figure that has grown so fabulous
There's not a neighbour left to say
When he finished his dog's day:
An ancient bankrupt master of this house.

Before that ruin came, for centuries,
Rough men-at-arms, cross-gartered to the
knees
Or shod in iron, climbed the narrow stairs,
And certain men-at-arms there were
Whose images, in the Great Memory stored,
Come with loud cry and panting breast

To break upon a sleeper's rest
While their great wooden dice beat upon the
board.

As I would question all, come all who can;
Come old, necessitous, half-mounted man;
And bring beauty's blind rambling
celebrant;
The red man the juggler sent
Through God-forsaken meadows; Mrs
French,
Gifted with so fine an ear;
The man drowned in a bog's mire,
When mocking muses chose the country
wench.

Did all old men and women, rich and poor,
Who trod upon these rocks or passed this
door
Whether in public or in secret, rage
As I do now against old age?
But I have found an answer in those eyes
That are impatient to be gone;
Go therefore; but leave Hanrahan
For I need all his mighty memories.

Old lecher with a love on every wind,
Bring up out of that deep considering mind
All that you have discovered in the grave,
For it is certain that you have
Reckoned up every unforeknown, unseeing

Plunge, lured by a softening eye,
Or by a touch or a sigh,
Into the labyrinth of another's being;

Does imagination dwell the most
Upon a woman won or woman lost?
If on the lost, admit you turned aside
From a great labyrinth out of pride,
Cowardice, some silly over-subtle thought
Or anything called conscience once;
And that if memory recur, the sun's
Under eclipse and the day blotted out.

III
It is time that I wrote my will;
I choose upstanding men
That climb the streams until
The fountain leap, and at dawn
Drop their cast at the side
Of dripping stone; I declare
They shall inherit my pride,
The pride of people that were
Bound neither to Cause nor to State,
Neither to slaves that were spat on,
Nor to the tyrants that spat,
The people of Burke and Grattan
That gave, though free to refuse –
Pride, like that of the morn,
When the headlong light is loose,
Or that of the fabulous horn,
Or that of the sudden shower

When all streams are dry,
Or that of the hour
When the swan must fix his eye
Upon a fading gleam,
Float out upon a long
Last reach of glittering stream
And there sing his last song.
And I declare my faith:
I mock Plotinus' thought
And cry in Plato's teeth,
Death and Life were not
Till man made up the whole,
Made lock, stock and barrel
Out of his bitter soul,
Aye, sun and moon and star, all,
And further add to that
That, being dead, we rise,
Dream and so create
Translunar Paradise.
I have prepared my peace
With learned Italian things
And the proud stones of Greece,
Poet's imaginings
And memories of love,
Memories of the words of women,
All those things whereof
Man makes a superhuman
Mirror-resembling dream.

As at the loophole there
The daws chatter and scream,

And drop twigs layer upon layer.
When they have mounted up,
The mother bird will rest
On their hollow top,
And so warm her wild nest.

I leave both faith and pride
To young upstanding men
Climbing the mountain-side,
That under bursting dawn
They may drop a fly;
Being of that metal made
Till it was broken by
This sedentary trade.

Now I shall make my soul,
Compelling it to study
In a learned school
Till the wreck of body,
Slow decay of blood,
Testy delirium
Or dull decrepitude,
Or what worse evil come –
The death of friends, or death
Of every brilliant eye
That made a catch in the breath –
Seem but the clouds of the sky
When the horizon fades;
Or a bird's sleepy cry
Among the deepening shades.

                7 October 1925

In this poem Yeats's mood is dramatically changed. Despite his recent Nobel Prize, senatorship, young family successful poetry and friends, he is quite suddenly suffering from depression, failure and fatigue. Suddenly for no obvious reason he feels physically very old. He talks directly for the first time about "this absurdity" his body, and his "troubled heart". He says that he "must bid the Muse go pack" because he has lost his ability to deal "in abstract things" and dare not express his feelings because he will "...be derided by / A sort of battered kettle at the heel". He knows he is sneered at, has become a laughing stock and is suddenly despised, but the circumstances that led to this are not explained.

The second stanza repeats social "ruin" and failing "foundations" with the "...tree, like a sooty finger..." pointing accusingly at him "under the day's declining beam'" The blackness of the soot and the twilight reveal that he feels dirtied, blackened by recent events, for which he holds himself responsible.

Yeats mentions a well-to-do neighbour, Mrs French, whose servants carried out illegal cruelty without her knowledge on her behalf, thinking she would condone it. Mrs French does not complain about this action or condemn it. He mentions also a peasant girl who has inadvertently caused deaths simply by being so beautiful and innocent. Men destroy themselves trying to impress her. Moon and sunlight was "one inextricable beam"; his wife and lover were both his loves, the legitimate one daylight and the illegitimate one moonlight.

The poet summons up all the dead, historical ghosts associated with the Tower including Mrs French, the peasant girl, Hanrahan, soldiers, a "halfmount" man and more, because he has a question to ask them. Subsequently he decides that only Hanrahan is necessary, "For I need all his mighty memories." Yeats says, "I myself created Hanrahan"; he takes full responsibility for anything Hanrahan says. This character from his drama is a red-haired schoolteacher of passionate intensity, who is unable to rest for eternity after his life is blighted by a fairy queen. Yeats sees him as another version of himself, since his own life has been similarly affected.

Just like Hanrahan, Yeats describes himself as a "half-mad rhapsodic poet, a failed seducer of real women and a great curser of old age". He is chased by "hounds", a "man drowned in a bog's mire / When mocking Muses chose the country wench." His wife George was a Londoner, and Maud Gonne and Iseult lived in Paris and Dublin; 'country wench' refers to Lily from County Carlow.

Like Hanrahan, Yeats, the "ancient bankrupt master of this house" has become "A lecher with a love on every wind" who has "reckoned up every unforeknown, unseeing / Plunge....Into the labyrinth of another's being": so this is the "... bog's mire..." that Yeats is referring to. Hanrahan knows about love affairs, and this is what Yeats needs advice about. His single urgent question is "Does the imagination dwell the most / On a woman won or a woman lost?" The "woman won" is George, who stayed with him despite his affair.

The time of writing tells us that the "woman lost" was Lily, for the poem was written just after her murder. "If [you decide] on the last [i.e. the woman lost]", continues Yeats, "admit you turned aside / From a great labyrinth out of pride, / Cowardice..." He had refused to become involved with his lover and son and now he is regretful and ashamed: "And if that memory recur, the sun's / Under eclipse and the day's blotted out...". He feels himself to blame for what occurred.

The grief that Yeats expressed so clearly and acutely is directed at a specific young woman after June 1925, as can be seen in "Colonus' Praise".

Colonus' Praise

Chorus: Come praise Colonus' horses, and come praise
The wine-dark of the wood's intricacies,
The nightingale that deafens daylight there,
If daylight ever visit where,
Unvisited by tempest or by sun,
Immortal ladies tread the ground
Dizzy with harmonious sound,
Semele's lad a gay companion.

And yonder in the gymnast's garden thrives
The self-sown, self-begotten shape that gives
Athenian intellect its mastery,
Even the grey-leaved olive tree
Miracle-bred out of the living stone;
Nor accident of peace or war
Shall wither that old marvel, for
The great grey-eyed Athena stares thereon.

Who comes into this country, and has come
Where golden crocus and narcissus bloom,
Where the Great Mother, mourning for her
daughter
And beauty-drunken by the water
Glittering among grey-leaved olive trees,
Has plucked a flower and sung her loss;
Who finds abounding Cephisus
Has found the loveliest spectacle there is.

Because this country has a pious mind
And so remembers that when all mankind
But trod the road, or splashed about the
shore,
Poseidon gave it bit and oar,
Every Colonus lad or lass discourses
Of that oar and of that bit;
Summer and winter, day and night,
Of horses and horses of the sea, white
horses.                              24    March
1927


This grief is further expressed in "A Man
Young and Old", the title of which judging
by the number of times he uses the word "I"
refers to himself.

A Man Young And Old
I

First Love

Though nurtured like the sailing moon
In beauty's murderous brood,
She walked awhile and blushed awhile
And on my pathway stood
Until I thought her body bore
A heart of flesh and blood.

But since I laid a hand thereon
And found a heart of stone
I have attempted many things
And not a thing is done,
For every hand is lunatic
That travels on the moon.

She smiled and that transfigured me
And left me but a lout,
Maundering here, and maundering there,
Emptier of thought
Than the heavenly circuit of its stars
When the moon sails out.
                    25 May 1926

   II
Human Dignity

Like the moon her kindness is,
If kindness I may call it,
What has no comphension in't,
But is the same for all

As though my sorrow were a scene
Upon a painted wall.

So like a bit of stone I lie
Under a broken tree.
I could recover if I shrieked
My heart's agony
To passing bird, but I am dumb
From human dignity.

1926 or 1927

III
The Mermaid

A mermaid found a swimming lad,
Picked him for her own,
Pressed his body to her body,
Laughed; and plunging down
Forgot in cruel happiness
That even lovers drown.

1926 or 1927

IV
The Death of the Hare

I have pointed out the yelling pack,
The hare leap into the wood,
And when I pass a compliment
Rejoice as lover should
At the drooping of an eye,
At the mantling of the blood.

Then suddenly my heart is wrung
By her distracted air
And I remember wildness lost
And after, swept from there,
Am set down standing in the wood
At the death of the hare.
                        January 1926

V
The Empty Cup

A crazy man that found a cup,
When all but dead of thirst,
Hardly dared to wet his mouth
Imagining, moom-accursed,
That another mouthful
And his beating heart would burst.
October last I found it too
But found it dry as bone,
And for that reason I am crazed
And my sleep is gone.
                        December 1926

VI
His Memories

We should be hidden from their eyes,
Being but holy shows
And bodies broken like a thorn
Whereon the bleak north blows,

To think of buried Hector
And that none living knows.

The women take so little stock
In what I do or say
They's sooner leave their cosseting
To hear a jackass bray;
My arms are like the twisted thorn
And yet there beauty lay;

The first of all the tribe lay there
And did such pleasure take –
She who had brought great Hector down
And put all Troy to wreck –
That she cried into this ear,
"Strike me if I shriek."
                              1926

VII
The Friends of His Youth

Laughter not time destroyed my voice
And put that crack in it,
And when the moon's pot-bellied
I get a laughing fit,
For that old Madge comes down the lane,
A stone upon her breast,
And a cloak wrapped about the stone,
And she can get no rest
With singing hush and hush-a-bye;
She that has been wild

And barren as a breaking wave
Thinks that the stone's a child.

And Peter that had great affairs
And was a pushing man
Shrieks "I am King of the Peacocks,"
And perches on a stone;
And then I laugh till tears run down
And the heart thumps at my side,
Remembering that her shriek was love
And that he shrieks from pride.
                    2 July 1926


VIII
Summer and Spring

We sat under an old thorn-tree
And talked away the night,
Told all that had been seen or done
Since first we saw the light,
And when we talked of growing up
Knew that we'd halved a soul
And fell the one in t'other's arms
That we might make it whole;
Then Peter had a murdering look,
For it seemed that he and she
Had spoken of their childish days
Under that very tree.
O what a bursting out there was,
And what a blossoming,
When we had all the summer-time

And she had all the spring!
                    1926


XI
The Secrets of the Old

I have old women's secrets now
That had those of the young;
Madge tells me what I dared not think
When my blood was strong,
And what had drowned a lover once
Sounds like an old song.

Though Margery is stricken dumb
If thrown in Madge's way,
We three make up a solitude;
For none alive today
Can know the secrets that we know
Or say the things we say;

How such a man pleased women most
Of all that are gone,
How such a pair loved many years
And such a pair but one,
Stories of the bed of straw
Or the bed of down.
                    1926 or 1927


X
His Wildness

O bid me mount and sail up there
Amid the cloudy wrack,
For Peg and Meg and Paris' love
That had so straight a back,
Are gone away, and some that stay
Have changed their silk for sack.

Were I but there and none to hear
I'd have a peacock cry,
For that is natural to a man
That lives in memory,
Being all alone I'd nurse a stone
And sing it lullaby.

1926

XI
From Oedipus at Colonus

Endure what life God gives and ask no
longer span;
Cease to remember the delights of youth,
travel-wearied aged man;
Delight becomes death-longing if all longing
else be vain.

Even from that delight memory treasures so,
Death, despair, division of families, all
entaglements of mankind grow,
As that old wandering beggar and these
God-hated children know.

In the long echoing street the laughing dancers throng,
The bride is carried to the bridegroom's chamber through torchlight and tumultuous song;
I celebrate the silent kiss that ends life short or long.

Never to have lived is best, ancient writers say,
Never to have drawn the breath of life, never to have looked into the eye of day;
The second best's a gay goodnight and quickly turn away.
    13 March 1927

In the first poem of the series, "First Love" this grief is for a girl who is dead, who "…blushed awhile…" and was as beautiful as "…the sailing moon…" She was "…In beauty's murderous brood…" meaning that beauty caused her downfall. (In early 20th century Ireland a pre-marital pregnancy would rob a beautiful young girl of respectability, future marriage and career; beauty could be a lifetime's curse.) In this poem, "Colonus' Praise" and "Human Dignity" Yeats refers to the girl as a "stone", "a scene upon a painted wall"; she is dead, only an image in his mind.

He describes his severe depression and longs to shout his grief aloud, "…but I am dumb / From human dignity". This "human dignity" that prevents him from uttering his grief is his only defence against "the yelling pack" he describes in the fourth poem, "The Death of the Hare". The hare - Lily - is a hunted, vulnerable creature, and the pack of hunting dogs finds its quarry at the end. He says he alerted the hare to the pack and to the safety of the wood – her change of name and address for anonymity - but he remembers "her distracted air". Now he has been "swept from there" and is no longer in contact with her, and is "set down standing in the wood / At the death of the hare." The wood signifies a place of safety from the pack of hounds, but also darkness, secrecy and illegality.

Poem five, "The Empty Cup" talks of water that had moistened him, made him fresh and young, until "his beating heart would burst". The lack of it has affected his health since "October last". He is now "dry as bone"; empty, lonely and grief-ridden.

In the first verse of poem six, "His Memories", he refers to himself and his wife as "holy shows" or painted ceremonial statues of "…bodies broken like a thorn /

Whereon the bleak north [wind] blows." They are both finding it difficult to keep face in public. He says he and George are like "buried Hector" of Greek mythology: once like Hector they were heroic, but both have now been publicly shamed by being dragged around the tomb of an enemy on chariot wheels, then slaughtered and buried. The dead enemy is Lily.

Nevertheless details of how they were degraded are not made public: " … none living knows". He remembers with real affection "…the first of all the tribe lay there…" in his arms, before "She    … brought great Hector down / And put all Troy to wreck … " He is again referring to Lily as Helen, who brought calamity to Troy inadvertently when she was wooed by Paris. Aphrodite, Greek goddess of love, promised him that Helen, wife of Menelaus, would be his wife. Helen in Greek legend was the most beautiful woman and the indirect cause of the Trojan war. She was daughter of Zeus, either by Leda or by Nemesis, and sister of the Dioscuri. From among her suitors she chose Menelaus, Agamemnon's younger brother, as her husband. However during his absence Helen fled to Troy with Paris. In "His Wildness" Yeats refers to himself as "Paris".

In the seventh poem, "The Friends of his Youth" the "laughter" in the first four lines is not mirth: it is the uncontrollable humourless laughter of madness or extreme grief, of being unable to come to terms with reality. He "...gets a laughing fit" "when the moon's pot-bellied"; when the moon is full he thinks of his dead lover, symbolised by darkness, the moon and extreme emotion.

Mrs Margaret Magill, a widow of forty-two with no children, was "...barren as a breaking wave..." in 1920 when Kevin was born. She lived in the cellar at 2, Catherine Street, Dublin with her partner James White and his son, Alfred. Lily had a room upstairs under the name of Lizzie O'Neill.

In 1922 Yeats moved back to Dublin from Oxford because the civil war was over. The Free State had been declared with much controversy because republicans did not want it, but Yeats was offered a place in government as a unionist senator. As it was paid work he was very happy to accept it. According to Brenda Maddox's biography of Yeats he was always short of money around this time.

He and George immediately moved from Oxfordshire to 83 Merrion Square, Dublin, and at the same time Lily also moved two streets away to 48 Newmarket Street. Yeats had already warned Lily that someone wanted to kill her and her child ("The Death of the Hare"), so at the same time she changed her name from 'Lizzie' to 'Honor Bright' and Kevin began to use his foster-mother's surname. He was subsequently raised as Margaret McGill's child rather than Lily's, and stayed at 2, Catherine Street as an anonymous working-class boy.

From the time that Lily was sacked from her job until the time of her murder she had financial help to pay for her and her son's upkeep and her son's foster-mother. In Dublin in the 1920s poor children went into the workhouse, but small children with more resources were often cared for by a foster-mother until socially presentable. Mrs Magill was a private nurse or midwife who had opted to care for one child only, and enough money was provided for her to look after Kevin full-time.

In "The Friends of his Youth" Yeats sees "...that old Madge come down the lane, / A stone upon her breast, / And a cloak wrapped about the stone..." She "...thinks the stone's a child..." and "Old Madge" or Margaret Magill "... can get no rest / with singing hush and hush-a-bye..." Once again Yeats is using Greek myth: Chronos, the Titan responsible for time, had many children by his wife Rhea; but her husband murdered them all at birth, believing they would overthrow him when older. Accordingly when Rhea became pregnant again she hid this child away, pretending to have a stone under her shawl rather than a live child. Chronos would laugh hysterically when he saw her. Meanwhile Zeus grew, eventually became King of the Gods and murdered his father. This poem shows Yeats's fear that his son Kevin would usurp his power, as well as his possessions.

Poem eight, "Summer and Spring" describes a meeting between two people in love. It does have a rural or park location but does not mention the seasons, so the title must refer to a meeting between partners in the spring and summer of life, disparate in age. When Kevin was born Yeats was fifty-five and Lily was twenty. He says they "... knew we'd halved a soul / And fell the one in t'other's arms / That we might make it whole ..."

Dublin in the mid 1920s was a small city with very little traffic. Everyone walked everywhere, whatever their status. Catherine Street was south east of the river Liffey off the Coombe, the main street in the Liberties. 48 Newmarket was marginally nearer to where Yeats and his family lived, in a big house in Merrion Square to the south-west near the government offices. The Abbey Theatre was just north of here, across the main bridge over the Liffey. When Yeats was visiting Dublin he resided at the St Stephen's Green Hibernian Club near the park, from where it was only 20 minutes walk to Lily's address.

Poem nine, "The Secrets of the Old", mentions Madge and Margery. Margaret Magill already knew Yeats, a tall, striking man, since she was looking after his son. Madge Hopkins, who had known Lily for five years at her death, knew both Yeats and Mrs Magill. After Lily's murder they will have continued to pass each other on the street; one can imagine looks and emotions exchanged. This puts the poem into context. As in poem seven Yeats has deliberately mixed up the names but they are recognisable: 'Madge' is Margaret Magill, and 'Margery' is Madge Hopkins who probably lived at 2 Catherine Street when

Kevin was born, and had the same address in Newmarket while Lily lived there as Honor Bright.

Yeats begins by saying he has "old women's secrets now, / That had them of the young." He means that Lily had told Margaret who was the father of her child. Margaret obviously spoke her mind to Yeats, for she had told him "...what I dared not think / When my blood was strong..." She probably intimated that one day he would not want to know his extra-marital lover or her illegitimate son, like most respectable married men. Mrs Magill had an accusing look for Madge Hopkins, who had contributed to Lily's death by inadvertently bringing her to a meeting called by her killer. When called to the witness box at the trial of Lily's alleged murderers, she had not given relevant evidence. Mrs McGill must have blamed her for this. She herself was not called as a witness, since the existence of a son was concealed. Hence "...Margery is stricken dumb / If thrown in Madge's way..." Yeats makes it clear that all three of them share a secret about a love affair between people of different social classes, one with "...the bed of straw..." and the other with the "...bed of down". He says "...We three make up a solitude: / For none alive today / Can know the stories that we know…"

# Yeats' remorse at the end of his life

In "Colonus' Praise" Yeats allows the chorus in his play "Oedipus at Colonus" to praise this town's "horses of the sea, white horses". These are wave crests ruled by the "bit and oar" donated to the town by Poseidon, God of the sea. In contrast to the whiteness of the waves, the wood is "wine-dark" like blood and "deafens daylight" "If daylight ever visit where, / Unvisited by tempest or by sun, / Immortal ladies tread the ground / Dizzy with harmonious sound..." In addition to grieving for the young dancer in the dark of the wood, the next verse shows that Yeats is also grieving for his own son, "the self-sown, self-begotten shape" ... /Miracle-bred out of the living stone" of his dead mother.

"The Winding Stair" shows the poet coming to terms with events. The actual winding stair in Thoor Ballylee led upwards in a spiral so one could not see far ahead, but at the top the broken walls revealed everything. Similarly in life each stage reveals more, but one only sees the whole picture at the end.

A Dialogue of Self and Soul

I

My Soul. I summon to the winding ancient stair;
Set all your mind upon the steep ascent,
Upon the broken, crumbling battlement,
Upon the breathless starlit air,
Upon the star that marks the hidden pole;
Fix every wandering thought upon
That quarter where all thought is done:
Who can distinguish darkness from the soul?

My Self. The consecrated blade upon my knee
Is Sato's ancient blade, still as it was,
Still razor-keen, still like a looking-glass
Unspotted by the centuries;
That flowering, silken, old embroidery, torn
From some court-lady's dress and round
The wooden scabbard bound and wound,
Can, tatted, still protect, faded adorn.

My Soul. Why should the imagination of a man
Log past his prime remember things that are
Emblematical of love and war?
Think of ancestral night that can,
If but imagination scorch the earth
And intellect its wandering
To this and that and t'other thing,

Deliver from the crime of death and birth.

My Self. Montashigi, third of his family,
fashioned it
Five hundred years ago, about it lie
Flowers from I know not what embroidery –
Heart's purple – and all these I set
For emblems of the day against the tower
Emblematical of the night,
And claim as by a soldier's right
A charter to commit the crime once more.

My Soul. Such fullness in that quarter
overflows
And falls into the basin of the mind
That man is stricken deaf and dumb and
blind,
For intellect no longer knows
Is from the Ought, or Knower from the
Known –
That is to say, ascends to Heaven;
Only the dead can be forgiven;
But when I think of that my tongue's a
stone.

II
My Self. A living man is blind and drinks
his drop.
What matter if the ditches are impure?
What matter if I live it all once more?
Endure that toil of growing up;

The ignominy of boyhood; the distress
Of boyhood changing into man;
The unfinished man and his pain
Brought face to face with his own
clumsiness;

The finished man among his enemies? –
How in the name of Heaven can he escape
That defiling and disfigured shape
The mirror of malicious eyes
Casts upon his eyes until at last
He thinks that shape must be his shape?
And what's the good of an escape
If honour find him in the wintry blast?

I am content to live it all again
And yet again, if it be life to pitch
Into the frog-spawn of a blind man's ditch,
A blind man battering blind men;
Or into that most fecund ditch of all,
The folly that man does
Or must suffer, if he woos
A proud woman not kindred of his soul.

I am content to follow to its source
Every event in action or in thought;
Measure the lot, forgive myself the lot!
When such as I cast out remorse
So great a sweetness flows into the breast
We must laugh and we must sing,
We are blest by everything,

Everything we look upon is blest.

July – December 1927

Yeats considers what will happen after his own death: "A man awaits his end / Dreading and hoping all…" In "A dialogue of Self and Soul" he contrasts "My Soul" or conscience with "My Self" or character. His soul summons him to "…the steep ascent…" towards the "…broken, crumbling battlement…" of "…the tower, / Emblematical of the night…" or Hell, for "Who can distinguish darkness from the soul?" Being deeply religious although not a church-goer, Hell is where he expects to pay for his crime: " …night … can …/ Deliver from the crime of death and birth." He accuses his Self of being confused about what "Is" done and what "Ought" to be done, and tells him he is guilty, for "Only the dead can be forgiven."

However Yeats's Self rises above religion, saying that he holds the sword with its embroidered scabbard of "heart's purple" as an emblem of good times and good deeds. He would "…claim as by a soldier's right / A charter to commit the crime once more." He argues that what he did to cause this grief was legitimate, and was worth doing, no matter what others think. In the second part he goes on to say "A living man is blind and drinks his drop. / What matter if the ditches are impure?" He clarifies this in the third stanza, "…That most fecund ditch of all, / … if he woos / A proud woman not kindred of his soul." He is referring to "The folly …" of having an affair with Lily.

In "Blood and the Moon" Yeats considers his tower and muses about the "…bloody, arrogant power" that built it, finally deciding "I declare this tower is my symbol…" because of its long history, the solidity of its thick walls, its winding staircase and the fact that it is "…half dead at the top…" as his own life now is.

Blood and the Moon
I
Blessed be this place,
More blessed still this tower;
A bloody, arrogant power
Rose out of the race
Uttering, mastering it,
Rose like these walls from these
Storm-beaten cottages –
In mockery I have set
A powerful emblem up,
And sing it rhyme upon rhyme
In mockery of a time
Half dead at the top.

II

Alexandria's was a beacon tower,  and Babylon's
An image of the moving heavens, a log-book of the sun's journey and the moon's;
And Shelley had his towers, thoughts crowned powers he called them once.

I declare this tower is my symbol; I declare
This winding, gyring, spiring treadmill of a stair is my ancestral stair;
That Goldsmith and the Dean, Berkeley and Burke have travelled there.

Swift beating on his breast in sybilline frenzy blind
Because the heart in his blood-sodden breast had dragged him down into mankind,
Goldsmith deliberately sipping at the honey-pot of his mind,

And haughtier-headed Burke that proved the State a tree,
That this unconquerable labyrinth of the birds, century after century,
Cast but dead leaves to mathematical equality;

And God-appointed Berkeley that proved all things a dream,

That this pragmatical, preposterous pig of a
world, its farrow that so solid seem,
Must vanish on the instant if the mind but
change its theme;

Saeva Indignatio and the labourer's hire,
The strength that gives our blood and state
magnanimity of its own desire;
Everything that is not God consumed with
intellectual fire.

III
The purity of the unclouded moon
Has flung its arrowy shaft upon the floor.
Seven centuries have passed and it is pure,
The blood of innocence has left no stain.
There, on blood-saturated ground, have
stood
Soldier, assassin, executioner,
Whether for pittance or in blind fear
Or out of abstract hatred, and shed blood,
But could not cast a single jet thereon.
Odour of blood on the ancestral stair!
And we that have shed none must gather
there
And clamour in drunken frenzy for the
moon.

IV
Upon the dusty, glittering windows cling,
And seem to cling upon the moonlit skies,

Tortoiseshell butterflies, peacock butterflies,
A couple of night-moths are on the wing.
Is every modern nation like the tower,
Half dead at the top? No matter what I said,
For wisdom is the property of the dead,
A something incompatible with life; and power,
Like everything that has the stain of blood,
A property of the living; but no stain
Can come upon the visage of the moon
When it has looked in glory from a cloud.
                                    August 1927

He talks of the moon, Lily's symbol, shining down on to the floor and revealing no bloodstains because "…the blood of innocence has left no stain." Meanwhile "…we that have shed none must gather there / And clamour in drunken frenzy for the moon." He regretted her loss and declared her innocent of the cause of her death.

He may also have regretted the false rumours of prostitution spread after her death by the police: "…No stain," he avers, "can come upon the visage of the moon…" The image of the moon as Lily is repeated in "The Crazed Moon" which is purportedly written in 1923. He sees the moon "…staggering…" after "…much child-bearing…" which causes her to be

"...despairing..." whilst we "...grope in vain / For children born of her pain". He talks of Lily as a child herself "...in all her virginal pride..." and the "...countryside..." where she grew up. The moonlight however is a "...malicious dream..." robbing all life from the flesh of his fingers and making them like skeletal claws ready to "...rend what comes in reach." It has turned him into a monster.

The Crazed Moon

Crazed through much child-bearing
The moon is staggering in the sky;
Moon-struck by the despairing
Glances of her wandering eye
We grope, and grope in vain,
For children born of her pain.

Children dazed or dead!
When she in all her virginal pride
First trod on the mountain's head
What stir ran through the country-side
Where every foot obeyed her glance!
What manhood led the dance!

Fly-catchers of the moon,
Our hands are blenched, our fingers seem
But slender needles of bone;
Blenched by that malicious dream

They are spread wide that each
May rend what comes in reach.
                April 1923

The conviction that he was culpable for
what had happened to Lily, though not for
her actual murder, remained with him for the
rest of his life and re-emerges with
regularity in other poems when he
speculates about his life after death. In
"Algeciras - A Meditation upon Death" he
compares his life to nightfall: "Greater glory
in the sun..." is his life of fame and success
on earth, whilst "An evening chill upon the
air..." has come upon his later life. Both of
these "Bid imagination run / Much on the
Great Questioner; / What He can question,
what if questioned I / Can with a fitting
confidence reply."

In "The Choice" he answers this conundrum
in saying "The intellect of man is forced to
choose / Perfection in the life or in the
work..." He has chosen work and "...the
day's vanity ..." which leads to "...the
night's remorse."

The Choice

The intellect of man is forced to choose
Perfection of the life, or of the work,

And if it takes the second must refuse
A heavenly mansion, raging in the dark.
When all that story's finished, what's the
news?
In luck or out the toil has left its mark:
That old perplexity an empty purse,
Or the day's vanity, the night's remorse.
February 1931

The series entitled "A Woman Young and
Old" is written just after Lily's death.
Whereas "A Man Young and Old" was
written from Yeats's point of view, this
series is written from Lily's point of view.

A Woman Young and Old
1929

I
Father and Child

She hears me strike the board and say
That she is under ban
Of all good men and women,
Being mentioned with a man
That has the worst of all bad names;
And thereupon replies
That his hair is beautiful,
Cold as the March wind his eyes.
1926

II

Before the World was made

If I make the lashes dark
And the eyes more bright
And the lips more scarlet,
Or ask if all be right
From mirror after mirror,
No vanity's displayed:
I'm looking for the face I had
Before the world was made.


What if I look upon a man
As though on my beloved,
And my blood be cold the while
And my heart unmoved?
Why should he think me cruel
Or that he is betrayed?
I'd have him love the thing that was
Before the world was made.
                    February 1928

III
A First Confession

I admit the briar
Entangled in my hair
Did not injure me;
My blenching and trembling
Nothing but dissembling,
Nothing but coquetry.

O long for truth, and yet
I cannot stay from that
My better self disowns,
For a man's attention
Brings such satisfaction
To the craving in my bones.
Brightness that I pull back
From the Zodiac,
Why those questioning eyes
That are fixed upon me?
What can they do but shun me
If empty night replies?
                    June 1927


IV
Her Triumph

I did the dragon's will until you came
Because I had fancied love a casual
Improvisation, or a settled game
That followed if I let the kerchief fall:
Those deeds were best that gave the minute
wings
And heavenly music if they gave it wit;
And then you stood among the dragon-rings.
I mocked, being crazy, but you mastered it
And broke the chain and set my ankles free,
Saint George or else a pagan Perseus;
And now we stare astonished at the sea,

And a miraculous strange bird shrieks at us.
                    20 November 1926

V
Consolation

O but there is wisdom
In what the sages said;
But stretch that body for a while
And lay down that head
Till I have told the sages
Where man is conforted.

How could passion run so deep
Had I never thught
That the crime of being born
Blackens all our lot?
But where the crime's committed
The crime can be forgot.
                    June 1927

VI
Chosen

The lot of love is chosen. I learnt that much
Struggling for an image on the track
Of the whirling zodiac.
Scarce did he my body touch,
Scarce sank he from the west
Or found a subterranean nest
On the maternal midnight of my breast

Before I had marked him on his northern
way,
And seemed to stand although in bed I lay.
I struggled with the horror of daybreak,
I chose it for my lot! If questioned on
My utmost pleasure with a man
By some new-married bride, I take
That stillness for a theme
Where his heart my heart did seem
And both adrift on the miracuous stream
Where – wrote a learned astrologer –
The Zodiac is changed into a sphere.
February 1926

VII
Parting

He. Dear, I must be gone
While night shuts the eyes
Of the household spies;
That song announces dawn.

She. No, night's bird and love's
Bids all true lovers rest,
While his loud song reproves
The murderous stealth of day.

He. Daylight already flies
From mountain crest to crest.

She. That light is from the moon.

He. That bird ...

She.          Let him sing on,
I offer to love's play
My dark declivities.
                    August 1926

VIII
Her Vision in the Wood

Dry timber under that rich foliage,
At wine-dark midnight in the sacred wood,
Too old for a man's love I stood in rage
Imagining men. Imagining that I could
A greater with a lesser pain assuage
Or but to find if withered vein ran blood,
I tore my body that its wine might cover
Whatever could recall the lip of lover.

And after that I held my fingers up,
Stared at the wine-dark nail, or dark that ran
Down every withered finger from the top;
But the dark changed to red, and torches
shone,
And deafening music shook the leaves; a
troop
Shouldered a litter with a wounded man,
Or smote upon the string and to the sound
Sang of the beast that gave the fatal wound.

All stately women moving to a song
With loosened hair or foreheads grief-
distraught,
It seemed a Quattrocento painter's throng,
A thoughtless image of Mantegna's thought
–

Why should they think that are forever
young?
Till suddenly in grief's contagion caught,
I stared upon his blood-bedabbled breast
And sang my malediction with the rest.

That thing all blood and mire, that beast-torn
wreck,
Half turned and fixed a glazing eye on mine,
And, though love's bitter-sweet had all
come back,
Those bodies from a picture or a coin
Nor saw my body fall nor heard it shriek,
Nor knew, drunken with singing as with
wine
That they had brought no fabulous symbol
there
But my heart's victim and its torturer.
                    August 1926


IX
A Last Confession

What lively lad most pleasured me

Of all that with me lay?
I answer that I gave my soul
And loved in misery,
But had great pleasure with a lad
That I loved bodily.

Flinging from his arms I laughed
To think his passion such
He fancied that I gave a soul
Did but our bodied touch,
And laughed upon his breast to think
Beast gave beast as much.

I gave what other women gave
That stepped out of their clothes,
But when this soul, its body off,
Naked to naked goes,
He it has found shall find therein
What none other knows,

And give his own and take hs own
And rule in his own right;
And though it loved in misery
Close and cling so tight,
There's not a bird of day that dare
Extinguish that delight.

                    June-August 1926

X
Meeting

Hidden by old age awhile
In masker's cloak and hood,
Each hating what the other loved,
Face to face we stood:
'That I have met with such," said he,
'Bodes me little good.'

'Let others boast their fill,' said I,
'But never dare to boast
That such as I had such a man
For lover in the past;
Say that of living men I hate
Such a man the most.'

'A loony'd boast of such a love,'
He in his rage declared:
But such as he for such as me –
Could we both discard
This beggarly habiliment –
Had found a sweeter word.

                    23 July – August 1926

XI
From the Antigone

Overcome – o bitter sweetness,
Inhabitant of the soft cheek of a girl –
The rich man  and his affairs,
The fat flocks and the field's fatness
Mariners, rough harvesters;
Overcome Gods upon Parnessaus;

Overcome the Empyrean; hurl
Heaven and Earth out of their places,
That in the same clamity
Brother and brother, friend and friend,
Family and family,
City and city may contend,
By that great glory driven wild.
Pray I will and sing I must,
And yet I weep – Oedipus' child
Descends into the loveless dust.
     15 September 1927 – February 1928

The first poem, "Father and Child" is said to have been written for Yeats's daughter Ann, who had fallen in love. It might also have been written for Lily on falling for an older man, and he may well have been addressing both young women simultaneously, since all other poems in this series are about Yeats' young lover. He warns her that people are shocked to hear who she is in love with, to which she replies "… That his hair is beautiful, / Cold as the March wind his eyes." She is so much in love that other people's opinions hold no weight.

This girl is very direct and independent of thought as can be seen in the second poem, where she is happy to attract any man. At the start of her life she innocently takes pleasure in sex as she says in "A First Confession". The "questioning eyes" of others do not bother her. In fact she has no relatives to warn her of problems to come.

In "Her Triumph" she admits she used to think love was "…a casual / Improvisation, or a settled game that followed if I let the kerchief fall…" But now she tells him she was a maiden amongst dragons, doing "…the dragon's will…" until he arrived "…And broke the chain and set the dragon free…" as if he were "…Saint George, or else a pagan Perseus". The sudden recognition of intense mutual attraction is eloquently depicted: "And now we stare astonished at the sea / And a miraculous strange bird shrieks at us." In "Consolation" the sharp pain of love is consoled by its consummation.

The sixth poem, "Chosen" is her sober realisation that he does not belong to her despite being with her overnight. He has chosen her as his lover and she has chosen him, but she must watch him go away every day when dawn appears.

Poem seven, "Parting" sees her persuading him to stay a little longer in the early morning. "He. Dear, I must be gone / While night shuts the eyes / Of the household spies; / That song announces dawn."

The eighth poem in this series depicts exactly the scene of Lily's murder. In "Her Vision in a Wood" a woman sees a murdered man, rather than a man a murdered woman; as in other poems Yeats has deliberately changed minor details. The location is the edge of a wood, a place of darkness and evil, and that is exactly where Lily's body was discovered, beside Ticknock wood. She was killed in the early hours of the morning or "wine-dark midnight". It was three days before his sixtieth birthday: "too old for a man"s love". On hearing the news of her death he "stood in rage imagining men".

Yeats apparently injured his body until it "ran blood...that its wine might cover whatever could recall the lip of lover." Nothing has been reported of this, since he disappeared from public view after her death due to "heart trouble" according to Joseph Hone in his biography of Yeats, published just after his death. "The dark turned to red, and torches shone..." as the body was discovered at dawn. Police and onlookers arrived, "And deafening music shook the leaves; a troop / Shouldered a litter with a

wounded man..." He stares at the corpse
"...though love's bitter-sweet had all come
back..." at the sight of "...my heart's victim
and its torturer". All the facts Yeats gives
about location, time of the assault and
activity of officials and onlookers had been
previously reported in newspapers.

In 1926 after visiting a school as a Senator
he wrote a poem about his dead lover and
their child. In "Among School Children" he
first sets the scene:

I walk through the long school-room
questioning;
A kind old nun in a white hood replies;
The children learn to cipher and to sing,
To study reading-books and history,
To cut and sew, be neat in everything
In the best modern way - the children's eyes
In momentary wonder stare upon
A sixty-year-old smiling public man.

He then pictures a scene in Lily's room one
evening, which reminded him of their
absolute affinity with each other:

 I dream of a Ledaean body, bent
Above a sinking fire, a tale that she
Told of a harsh reproof, or trivial event
That changed some childish day to tragedy -

Told, and it seemed that our two natures
blent
Into a sphere from youthful sympathy,
Or else, to alter Plato's parable,
Into the yolk and white of the one shell.

Having established the depth of their
relationship he remembers her moods and
features, and tries to find them in the
children in front of him. Although she was
so beautiful, her child may be
indistinguishable to him, so he does his best
to remember her face:

And thinking of that fit of grief or rage
I look upon one child or t'other there
And wonder if she stood so at that age -
For even daughters of the swan can share
Something of every paddler's heritage -
And had that colour upon cheek or hair,
And thereupon my heart is driven wild:
She stands before me as a living child.

He is so moved by her image in his mind
and by the recent aging of his own
appearance that he is almost in tears, but he
struggles with his outward expression to
make it acceptable to those around him:

Her present image floats into the mind -
Did Quattrocento finger fashion it

Hollow of cheek as though it drank the wind
And took a mess of shadows for its meat?
And I though never of Ledaean kind
Had pretty plumage once - enough of that,
Better to smile on all that smile, and show
There is a comfortable kind of old
scarecrow.

Thinking about a young mother with a child
made him remember his own mother: would
she be happy with the result of her labour
sixty years later? Would his own mother or
Lily think that giving birth to a son had been
worthwhile? Would her son's life be what
she wanted for him?

What youthful mother, a shape upon her lap
Honey of generation had betrayed,
And that must sleep, shriek, struggle to
escape
As recollection or the drug decide,
Would think her son, did she but see that
shape
With sixty or more winters on his head,
A compensation for the pang of his birth,
Or the uncertainty of his setting forth?

Plato thought nature but a spume that plays
Upon a ghostly paradigm of things;
Solider Aristotle played the taws
Upon the bottom of a king of kings;

World-famous golden-thighed Pythagoras
Fingered upon a fiddle-stick or strings
What a star sang and careless muses heard:
Old clothes upon old sticks to scare a bird.

Nuns worship abstract images rather than flesh and blood, but both statues and children represent heaven on earth:

Both nuns and mothers worship images,
But those the candles light are not as those
That animate a mother's reveries,
But keep a marble or a bronze repose.
And yet they too break hearts - O Presences
That passion, piety or affection knows,
And that all heavenly glory symbolise -
O self-born mockers of man's enterprise;

Yeats finally says that this new child is growing freely, unlike his parents. He will not experience guilt leading to bodily harm, or beauty as a result of pain, or hours spent writing out poems at night:

Labour is blossoming or dancing where
The body is not bruised to pleasure soul,
Nor beauty born out of its own despair,
Nor blear-eyed wisdom out of midnight oil.

The child he and Lily have produced is like part of a chestnut tree; if the leaf it will last a season and wither away; if the blossom it will have a happy life and may produce seed for next season; if the bole or trunk it will provide many descendants for generations He ends with a question: how can we identify our passion in the flesh? How can he identify his son by Lily?

 O chestnut tree, great-rooted blossomer,
Are you the leaf, the blossom or the bole?
O body swayed to music, O brightening glance,
How can we know the dancer from the dance?

This poem shows clearly that Yeats suffered emotionally from Lily's unexpected absence and felt bereft at losing contact with his son. This deep grief lasted for around three years judging from the other poems written around this period.

The final three poems in "A Woman Young and Old" say what Lily thought about their hopeless predicament of being illicit lovers with unacceptable differences in social class, money, religion and politics as well as age. In "A Last Confession" she says she "…gave my soul and loved in misery…" She looks forward to the time when his soul, "…its body off…" finds hers, and discovers

"…what none other knows…", her love for him. He will then be free of earthly bonds and able to "give his own and take his own / And rule in his own right."

"Meeting" describes the differences between the two lovers. He was "Hidden by old age…" and disguised "…in masker's cloak and hood…" They had differences of opinion, "Each hating what the other loved…" and he could see no advantage in their union, saying that it "…bodes me little good." It was no love to boast of, although they "…had found a sweeter word…" The major problem however was "…this beggarly habiliment…" of social and class constraints.

This is the note Yeats ends on in "From the Antigone" where he asks the powers that create the "Bitter sweetness, inhabitant of the soft cheek of a girl" to "Overcome the Empyrean", to shake up and demolish the customary social divisions that pit people against each other. "Pray I will and sing I must…" he says, but he cannot prevent "Oedipus's' child…" - the product of an impermissible alliance from sinking "…into the loveless dust."

As a lapsed Christian he feels that he can no longer look forward to heaven on death. He admits that he has caused this great tragedy by loving Lily and his first son and by creating his wife's jealousy, as can be seen in the following poem. (He does not mention his wife's or O'Higgin's culpability, malice or criminal actions.)

At Algeciras – A Meditation upon Death

The heron-billed pale cattle-birds
That feed on some foul parasite
Of the Moroccan flocks and herds
Cross the narrow Straits to light
In the rich midnight of the garden trees
Till the dawn break upon those migled seas.

Often at evening when a boy
Would I carry to a friend –
Hoping more substantial joy
Did an older mind commend –
Not such as are in Newton's metaphor,
But actual shells of Rosses' level shore.

Greater glory in the sun,
An evening chill upon the air,
Bid imagination run
Much on the Great Questioner;
What He can question, what if questioned I
Can with a fitting confidence reply.

**\*\*\*\*\*\*\*\***

'William Butler Yeats and Honor Bright'
Series:

1.    W. B. Yeats and the Murder of
Honor Bright

2.    An Analysis of Selected Poetry by
William Butler Yeats between 1918 and
1928

3.    Who Killed Honor Bright?
     How William Butler and George
Yeats Caused the Fall of the Irish Free
State

www.ingramcontent.com/pod-product-compliance
Lightning Source LLC
Chambersburg PA
CBHW070833100426
42813CB00003B/595